Original title:
The Starfish's Dream

Copyright © 2025 Creative Arts Management OÜ
All rights reserved.

Author: Christian Leclair
ISBN HARDBACK: 978-1-80587-269-6
ISBN PAPERBACK: 978-1-80587-739-4

## Radiance at the Water's Edge

Once a starfish wore a crown,
Sparkling bright, it swam around.
With seashells dancing on its head,
It claimed, "I reign!" with joy it said.

A jellyfish said, "That's quite absurd,
You can't be king, you lack a bird!"
The starfish laughed, "I'll prove you wrong,
With ocean songs and dances strong!"

It frolicked near the sandy shore,
Where crabs joined in, a lively score.
With tiny pails, they built a castle,
Each flopped about, a happy hassle!

But seagulls laughed and swooped down low,
"Your crown's just sand, and quite a show!"
Yet our starfish chuckled, waved a limb,
"Let them laugh, it's still a whim!"

So they danced till the sun hit the sea,
In splashes of laughter, wild and free.
For a kingdom made of joy and sand,
Is worth much more than a seagull's brand!

## **Whispers of a Tidal Night**

Beneath the moon's soft gleam,
A starfish sings, or so it seems,
With jellyfish as its dancing crew,
They sway in blue, oh what a view!

Crabs tap their claws in rhythmic beats,
While seaweed sways in lively feats,
"Hey, look at me!" a fishy shouts,
As bubbles float and laughter sprouts.

## Secrets Beneath the Waves

An octopus plays hide and seek,
In a coral home, not so bleak,
With eight long arms, it twists and turns,
While other fish just watch and yearn.

A clam then boasts, "I'm shy, you see,"
But gleams like gold, quite clumsily,
"Don't judge my style, it's all the rage!"
As tides roll in, they laugh off stage.

## Echoes of the Ocean Floor

A sea turtle rolls a disco ball,
Inviting all to join the call,
With seahorses twirling side to side,
In the underwater, fun-ride tide.

A dolphin leaps with joyful yelps,
As fish create a conga kelp,
"Keep up, slowpokes!" they all chime in,
With waves of laughter, they begin to spin.

## **Luminescent Journeys**

Starfish wear hats, it's quite the sight,
Dancing under bioluminescent light,
They laugh and spin, a quirky scene,
   In hues of green, oh so serene!

A whale nearby jokes with its song,
"Join my party, you can't go wrong!"
With bubbles and sparkles in the air,
The ocean's humor is hard to compare.

## **Surrendering to the Currents of Time**

A starfish launched on a lazy spree,
Waves giggle softly, oh so carefree.
Caught in a whirlpool of seaweed spins,
It waves at the fish, where the fun begins.

Sunburned shells play a melody sweet,
Chubby crabs dance in a jubilant beat.
Bubbles pop with a comedic sound,
While seagulls swoop, they're feet off the ground.

The boardwalk's a stage, a beachy parade,
With jellyfish twirling, oh what has been made!
Salt in the air and a wink from the tide,
A starfish grins wide, it's just along for the ride.

Time drifts like sand, without a care,
As waves tickle toes in a sun-kissed affair.
A laugh on the breeze, a giggle on shore,
Our starfish is dreaming, wanting nothing more.

# Beneath the Veil of Foam

Under the foamy, bubbly embrace,
A starfish wears seaweed like a lace.
Giggling mollusks, with shells on their backs,
Perform synchronized waltzes, no room for slack.

Waves wash in secrets, shrouded in glee,
With crabs as the dancers, all wild and free.
The sea's like a circus, all splashy and bright,
As fish wear their smiles, a colorful sight.

The starfish twirls like it's showing off,
While ticklish tides join in with a scoff.
"Hey, look at me, I've got eight arms to spare!"
And says with a wink, "Who needs a care?"

Through bubbles and sprays, joy weaves its spell,
In the ocean's grand stories, we know it so well.
Laughter and splashes, all swimming in tune,
Life's just a party beneath the bright moon.

## Mosaic Dreams in Salty Air

Colors collide, a palette divine,
A starfish grins, sipping seaweed wine.
Jellyfish giggles, floating by chance,
While clams and mussels all join in the dance.

The surf splashes laughter, it echoes above,
As gulls drop jokes, a comedic love.
With shells as their instruments, they play a song,
The starfish sings loud, "Come join us, come along!"

Sunset paints whispers, a shimmering spree,
Dancing above, the bright lights at sea.
A canvas of bubbles, swirling like dreams,
With every loud laugh, the whole ocean beams.

Waves tumble over in playful delight,
As creatures unite in the fading light.
Each ripple a chuckle, a splash, and a cheer,
Mosaic dreams formed, where joy disappears.

## Driftwood Stories from the Deep

Once upon driftwood, a tale set sail,
With starfish narrating, it's bound to prevail.
The octopus laughs, and the pufferfish grins,
As they tell of the times they flew with the fins.

A crab with a top hat takes center stage,
With sea cucumbers, in plays of great wage.
"Historical tales of tides once so grand,
And how we all danced at the driftwood band!"

In the murmurs of sea foam, tales weave and twist,
Each character chuckles in a frothy mist.
Bubbles giggle softly, riding the seas,
As waves carry stories, all shifting with ease.

The current hums songs of laughter and glee,
Where starfish share dreams, so fun and so free.
So grab a driftwood, and stay for a while,
In the ocean's grand book, let's dive in with style!

## Towards the Horizon of Wonder

A starfish sat with dreams so wide,
It stared at waves on the ocean side.
With wishes grand and a wishful grin,
It hoped to sail where the sea began.

It told a crab, "I'll fly one day!"
"With flippers and a plan, away I'll sway!"
The crab just laughed, no fear of heights,
While planning underwater pizza nights.

"But wait!" squealed clam, "You'll need a boat!"
"Or maybe just some seaweed to float!"
They built a craft from shells and glee,
With smooth ideas swimming wild and free.

But when they launched, the boat turned fast,
And starfish found itself stuck in the mast.
"Oh dear!" it sighed, "I float too high!"
It limped back home; dreams washed away to dry.

## The Untold Stories of the Tides

In tidal tales told by the sea,
Lived a starfish who danced with glee.
It twirled with shells, in underwater light,
Claiming each wave was a dazzling flight.

"I'll dazzle fish with my finest moves!"
The fish just rolled its skeptical grooves.
"Do fish even dance?" a seahorse cracked.
"Let's see this starfish, its talent unpacked!"

With a flip and a twist, it caught a wave,
The ocean chuckled, so cheeky and brave.
"More like a flap than a dance, you see!"
But laughter echoed, as fun set them free.

And when left alone, with the sun going down,
The sea hummed soft, no trace of a frown.
For stories told under silver moon light,
Brought tides of laughter and joy overnight.

## Between the Stars and Seafoam.

A starfish wished to reach the sky,
With seafoam dreams, it gave a try.
"I'll jump so high and tickle the stars!"
It practiced by flipping on passing cars.

Each splash of foam sparked a laugh,
As it wobbled round on the bubbly path.
"What a sight!" said a gull up above,
"A starfish aspiring, how sweet is that love!"

But the gleaming twinkle of stars so bright,
Moved far too fast for a flip at night.
The waves just giggled, the bubbles did burst,
While the starfish pondered its dreams first.

Finally it said, "I'll stick to the sea,"
"For stars are best left where they should be."
And with a splash, it found perfect cheer,
Dancing in foam, the sky feeling near.

## Celestial Whispers in Tidal Pools

Down in a pool, so calm and bright,
A starfish plotted its escape from night.
"I'll chat with the moon, share a joke or two,"
"And teach it to dance, as all friends do!"

Among the pebbles, it tossed and turned,
While the moon blinked down, the tides discerned.
"What's a starfish in the dark without light?"
"I need a punchline, a giggle to excite!"

The shrimp on the side piped up with glee,
"Tell it a riddle, like who's smarter, me?"
"You can't count shrimp!" the starfish grew bold,
"But dreams are silly, a truth to be told!"

So off it went, to find its bright friend,
With jokes to share and laughter to blend.
And in the pool, where stars softly lay,
The whispers echoed, "Let's dance 'til day!"

# A Luminous Journey Beneath the Waves

In the deep, where the bubbles rise,
A fish tells tales with big, wide eyes.
With laughter echoing through the blue,
He dances around, saying, "Join my crew!"

Clams clap shells like they're in a band,
With octopuses waving all over the sand.
A sea turtle winks, offers a ride,
While jellyfish glow, their humor can't hide.

Anemones giggle with ticklish delight,
As seahorses prance, oh, what a sight!
Together they spin, losing their cares,
In this marvelous world, down the ocean stairs.

A shrimp cracks jokes, the crowd is in stitches,
While crabs do the cha-cha, with sassy glitches.
A luminous journey, so wild and free,
In the waves of laughter, we all just be!

## **Echoes of the Forgotten Shore**

At the shore where the whispers play,
Old shells gossip about yesterday.
A crab in a top hat sips on some tea,
While sea gulls squawk a comedy spree.

Drifting tides bring a curious crowd,
A starfish shimmies, oh so proud.
He claims he once danced with a mermaid fair,
But no one believes, they just stare and stare.

Seaweed sways, sharing tall tales,
Of treasures lost and legendary gales.
The sand's a stage, the waves applaud,
While the ocean unfolds its quirky façade.

With laughter erupting, the tide's taking bets,
On which fish will win in the funny fish sets.
Echoes of laughter, like bubbles that rise,
On the forgotten shore, under bright sunny skies.

## Stardust on the Seabed

Amidst the coral, stories unfold,
Of quirky critters and treasures untold.
A pufferfish wearing a fancy hat,
Declares he's the king, just look at that!

Worms do the worm in the glittering sand,
While a clam tries to dance, isn't it grand?
A tour guided by sea urchins so wise,
With jokes that sparkle like bright starlit skies.

The sea stars grin, with limbs all akimbo,
They're masters of fun, just watch them go!
With bubbles of laughter floating up high,
This stardust below will make your heart fly.

The party keeps rolling, vibrant and bright,
As fish tell puns that tickle the night.
Stardust dazzles, while creatures delight,
In this underwater carnival, pure and light.

## Beneath the Ocean's Velvet Veil

Under the waves, where the colors twirl,
A ticklish octopus begins to swirl.
With prosthetic legs and a grin so wide,
He invites all the fish to take a ride!

Beneath the velvet, mischief brews,
A sea lion juggles, making the news.
Turtles just chuckle, they're wise and slow,
While dolphins leap high, putting on a show.

Fish play charades with bubbles for clues,
And the sea cucumbers share wacky views.
An urchin with shades claims he's the best,
In the court of the sea, he's passed every test.

Giggles and splashes fill the bright tide,
Where silliness blooms, and joy cannot hide.
Beneath the ocean, what a playful veil,
In this realm of laughter, we set sail!

## Fantasies of a Sandy Soul

In a shell, I found a throne,
With a crown made of sea foam.
I ruled the waves, quite feeling grand,
Till a crab claimed it—oh, how unplanned!

I dreamed of pearls and tasty treats,
But seaweed wrapped 'round my feet.
I tried to dance on waves so high,
Ended up singing to the sky!

Fish threw parties, full of glee,
They asked me to join; I had to flee.
The sea cucumbers stole my style,
While jellyfish laughed all the while!

But in my heart, a joy so sly,
Sandy soul, I'll reach for the sky!
With every splash, a giggle spills,
Oh, the ocean is full of thrills!

## Ocean's Secret Serenade

A clam opened up to sing a tune,
While dolphins danced 'neath the moon.
I joined in, a solo quite absurd,
My notes got lost in the sea breeze heard!

The octopus played a banjo fake,
While turtles laughed till they'd shake.
A whale in the back gave a grand sigh,
Said, "Not my style, can't deny!"

And every starfish found a voice,
Made a band—it was our choice.
With bubbles popping all around,
Our secret songs were quite profound!

A playful splash, a joyful cheer,
In this watery world, we have no fear.
Just sing along, it's coral time,
With giggles shared in every rhyme!

## A Dance Among the Coral Lights

Beneath the waves, where colors gleam,
I joined the fish in a silly dream.
Their scales sparkled, a disco ball,
While I just flopped—oh, not so small!

Sea anemones swayed with flair,
I tried to twirl but lost my hair.
A sea horse said, "You've got some moves!"
But I just wiggled, no fancy grooves!

A crab showed off his sideway slide,
While I rolled over—oh, I can't hide!
The coral laughed, in hues so bright,
As I danced clumsily through the night!

Yet in this dance, I found my way,
Swayed by laughter, brightening the day.
So here we twirl, a motley crew,
In ocean's glow, just me and you!

## Dreams Drifting on Briny Breezes

I dreamt of sailing on a fishy boat,
With seaweed sails, oh, how they float!
But the fish were stubborn, wouldn't row,
Instead, they just put on a show!

The jellyfish wore fancy hats of blue,
Said, "Join our party; it's a must-do!"
So I flopped in, feeling quite spry,
Till a wave took me—Oh my, oh my!

I floated past a crabby old king,
Who said, "You can't dance; you've lost your zing!"
I waved my arms, gave a goofy grin,
They fell for my charm and let me in!

On briny breezes, we sang and laughed,
Turning every wave into a craft.
So here's to dreams that swirl and spin,
In the ocean's heart, let the fun begin!

## A Voyage to Tranquil Realms

In a boat made of jellybeans,
My friends sing silly tunes,
Bouncing waves of rainbow hues,
Chasing laughs beneath the moons.

We roped a fish with funny hats,
He danced like he had no cares,
With bubbles bursting into chats,
And jelly squids doing square pairs.

The lanterns glowed with candy lights,
While crabs played cards 'til late,
What a sight of pure delight,
In a world that laughs at fate.

Oh what joy on this wild night,
Where even seashells join the fun,
Every splash is pure delight,
Until the dawn brings up the sun!

## Melodies from Distant Shores

A turtle strummed a ukulele,
With rhythm that could make you sway,
While seagulls joined in like a band,
Singing songs of a sunny day.

The dolphins did a wiggly dance,
With moves that made the waves all giggle,
Each flip a splash of jolly chance,
As seaweed swayed, oh so wiggle.

Octopuses tapping their feet,
Grooving in shades of bright turquoise,
The ocean floor was such a treat,
With laughter ringing like their voice.

So come and join this silly crowd,
Where every fish has got a song,
In waters deep and vibrant loud,
The joy of waves will carry on!

## Spirits of the Deep Blue

Ghostly fish with glittery tails,
Haunting corals in a spooky light,
They giggle softly with ghostly wails,
As mermaids chuckle through the night.

A crab in disguise as a pirate bold,
With a treasure chest full of old shoes,
He tells tall tales of the brave and the cold,
While friendly sharks play peek-a-boo blues.

An octopus with nine different hats,
Exclaims he's the king of this place,
But all the fish just roll their mats,
And laugh at his oversized grace.

So if you dive into this sea,
Beware of giggles and ocean pranks,
For laughter flows as wild and free,
Among the quirky ocean ranks!

## The Color of Ocean's Reverie

A fish with stripes of boldest hues,
Painted bright from tail to fin,
Swam with style, spreading the news,
That splashy smiles always win!

A rainbow wave rolled into view,
With cotton candy clouds on top,
The seagulls sang a sticky tune,
As jellyfish spun, they just won't stop.

Each wave was a giggle, a frolic, a tease,
With seashells sharing their silly rhymes,
Making pearls of laughter with easy ease,
In this place where joy always climbs.

So dive into this ocean's art,
And let the colors make you beam,
For here's a world, a comic heart,
Where fun and laughter weave the dream!

## Echoes of the Sea's Secrets

In the tide's gentle sigh, they sing,
A clam with a hat, what a funny thing!
Starfish hold court, with shells as their chairs,
Crabs doing the cha-cha, showing off pairs.

The kelp tickles fish, who giggle in glee,
One waved to a wave, "Hey, come dance with me!"
Jellyfish bounce like balloons of delight,
With dreams of a party beneath the moonlight.

A dolphin pops by, flipping with flair,
"Who knew the ocean could have such a air?"
An octopus paints with its colorful ink,
Creating a mural of what we can think.

And as the tides chant their watery jokes,
The seaweed shakes back, with giggles and pokes.
At night when the stars twinkle bright from afar,
The sea swirls in laughter, beneath the same star.

## **Stardrops on Soft Shores**

On sandy shores where laughter grows,
A clam said, "Why not wear some clothes?"
Seagulls gossip with wind-blown flair,
While crabs juggle shells, split in mid-air.

Stars twinkle down, casting giggles below,
As starfish share tales of the tides' ebb and flow.
'Once I was flipped by a wave oh so bold!'
They laugh as the night whispers secrets untold.

Seashells collect stories, each one unique,
Of mermaids who wobbled and fish that can squeak.
A chorus of bubbles, a bubbling cheer,
In the ocean's vast playground, there's nothing to fear.

With moonlight as music, they twirl and tease,
Under the watch of the stars and the breeze.
A world full of joy, that's born from the foam,
Where every wave whispers, 'This is our home!'

## A Canvas of Uncharted Waters

In waters where colors dance and play,
A starfish stumbles on paint, what a day!
Brushes made of seaweed, colors from shells,
Creating great art, as laughter compels.

Wave after wave, they splash about,
The crabs critique, while the fish all pout.
"No talent for critters!" the dolphin did croon,
As they painted the ocean, under the moon.

Each twirl on the canvas sent ripples of fun,
An octopus winks, "Look what we've done!"
A gallery opening, right by the reef,
Sea creatures admiring with bubbles of grief.

So here in the blue, they knit dreams with flair,
In a world where each stroke's a splash of rare air.
And under the starlight, they all grow giddy,
A masterpiece born from their oceanic city.

## Musings of the Deep Blue

In the ocean's embrace, the fish start to jest,
A star with a grin says, "I'm better than the rest!"
Turtles wear glasses, debating the light,
While waves do a dance under moonshine so bright.

An oyster makes pearls, with a flick and a flair,
Claiming, "I'm fancy, with my jewels to wear!"
But a wise little shrimp, with a wink and a nod,
Says, "Beauty is fleeting, you're still just a clod!"

The dolphins share puns, their laughter like bells,
As the sea cucumbers spin oceanic tales.
With each rising tide, new jokes soft and clear,
In waters so deep, there's nothing to fear.

So in the blue depths, let giggles arise,
Dancing with moonbeams, sparkling like eyes.
Together they float, in a whimsical spree,
The musings of the ocean, forever carefree.

## Fantasies Among Sea Anemones

In a world of squishy splendor,
Dance with colors bright and tender.
Pinky fingers wave with glee,
Tickling fish, oh what a spree!

Jellyfish wearing crowns of lace,
Giggling shrimps all over the place.
Octopuses playing hide and seek,
In a sea of humor, none are meek.

Synchronized swimming by clumsy crab,
Clapping fins, what a noisy fab!
Seaweed swaying to their glee,
Join the laughter, can you see?

In this oceanic circus delight,
Fishes fly, what a funny sight!
Anemones cheer, their wishes grand,
A comedy show, unplanned but well planned!

# **Embraced by the Moonlit Tides**

Under the moon, waves splash and play,
A clam sings tunes as bright as day.
Starry-eyed turtles take a bow,
Surprised by their own fanciful wow!

Crabs in tuxedos dance with flair,
Flipping and flopping without a care.
Lobsters boast of their fancy shells,
While coral giggles, oh what a swell!

Fishes wearing shades, they strut,
Chasing shadows in a little nut.
The tides encourage a rare ballet,
As all of Ocean's quirky join the fray!

With laughter echoing through the deep,
Not a single soul would dare to sleep.
Mocking currents, moonlit pride,
Makes waves of joy, none can abide!

# **Currents of Hope in Saltwater**

A sardine's joke, oh so fishy,
Makes everyone feel quite squishy.
As bubbles pop in glee nearby,
Clams laugh hard, they're on a high!

Little sea stars throw a party,
With disco lights, it gets quite hearty.
Mussels jam with a jazzy twist,
Creating rhythms that can't be missed!

The dolphins prank with splashy flair,
Chasing shadows, do you dare?
Seahorses jive, all fancy and cool,
While creatures gather, break all the rules!

In salty waves, hopes flow and sway,
A festival of fun where all can play.
With laughter rippling beneath each tide,
The ocean's heart is open wide!

## Following the Path of the Sea

On a jellyfish, I jump and glide,
Sailing easy like the tide.
Sandy shores with jokes in tow,
Crabs clap to the rhythm's flow!

Schooling fish tell tales so tall,
About the one that almost had a ball.
Starfish giggle, they spin just so,
Waving eight arms to steal the show!

Barnacles dressed for the masquerade,
Join a conch playing serenade.
The sea is a stage, come take a seat,
Where every wave makes life a treat!

With the ocean's laughs, we follow the map,
In this watery world, take a joyful snap.
With fins and flippers, we're all in free,
Chasing dreams through watery spree!

## The Heartbeat of Deep-Water Wishes

In the ocean's embrace, they wiggle and sway,
Tiny wishes afloat, hoping to play.
A fish with a tickle, a crab with a dance,
They giggle and bubble, lost in romance.

With dreams of a treasure, they search for a pearl,
But stumble on seashells and whirls that twirl.
A dolphin's cartwheel, a whale's giant grin,
Their laughter echoes, the fun's about to begin.

Little jellyfish spin, like ballerinas bright,
They twirl in the currents, oh, what a sight!
A hermit crab chuckles as he dons a new home,
In mismatched shells, he feels free to roam.

With every wave that crashes and glints,
The heartbeat of wishes laughs and hints.
So dive into this whimsy where no one will frown,
In the depths of the sea, we're never alone!

## **Visions Carried by the Wind**

A seagull croaks loudly, with style so grand,
It claims all the snacks on the soft golden sand.
While crabs scuttle sideways, they dance on their toes,
In the theater of waves, where the sea breeze blows.

The starfish wears shades, quite a sight to behold,
Sunning on rocks, feeling oh so bold.
But with every small gust, he tumbles around,
Shouting, "Hey, keep it easy, I'm trying to lounge!"

Fish flinging confetti, what a colorful scheme,
They scatter in bubbles, like clouds in a dream.
Each splash is a giggle, a story well spun,
In this ocean of laughter, the tides are all fun!

As visions sail softly on the light, balmy breeze,
They twirl and they flip, like leaves on the trees.
So come dip your toes in this whimsical land,
Where every small whisper of waves is well planned!

## A Sea of Endless Possibilities

Beneath waves of giggles, the world opens wide,
With krill playing hide-and-seek in the tide.
Octopuses juggle—such talent, oh my!
While turtles fly by in their dreams, oh so spry!

"Why don't we all dance?" a clownfish demands,
As they spin on the coral, in colorful bands.
A conch joins the party, but gets dizzy, oh dear,
And rolls down the reef with a small squeaky cheer.

With bubbles as balloons, they float in the sun,
Every day's a carnival—oh, what fun!
Seahorses prance with their best pals in tow,
While the ocean sings loud, putting on a show.

In this sea of wonders, where laughter is free,
The possibilities stretch, just like the deep sea.
So hop in your flippers, dance, wiggle, and sway,
Join this underwater bash—come play, hip hooray!

## Emerging from the Shell

Out of a shell with a hesitant peek,
A tiny new creature decides to speak.
"Is it safe to come out? Will the world be bright?"
A crab in a tux gives a wink of goodnight.

The curious hermit, oh what shall he wear?
As he tries on new homes, he gives them a stare.
"Too big or too small, it just doesn't fit,
But I'll strut my stuff, oh I won't throw a fit!"

And there at the bottom, the deep secrets swam,
Giggling sea urchins, each dressed like a glam.
With pearls for the crown, they host a grand fest,
To welcome young holders and put them to the test!

Taking risks with a splash and a bound,
Emerging with laughter—that's what's profound!
So come share in the joy, where sea meets the shell,
For growth brings both giggles, oh can't you tell?

## Castles Built in the Sand

Along the shore, we sculpt our fate,
A drippy tower, oh what a state!
A crab walks by, gives us a stare,
"Your sandy castle? I don't care!"

Seagulls laugh with feathers so bright,
As waves come crashing, oh what a sight!
Our dreams get washed away in the foam,
But still, we giggle, this is our home.

# **Dreams of Twilight Waters**

Under the glow of the moon's soft light,
Fish wear pajamas, what a silly sight!
Octopuses dance with eight left feet,
While turtles tap on the ocean's beat.

Mermaids giggle, their hair in a twirl,
Serving seaweed smoothies, oh what a whirl!
As whispers of laughter fill the sea,
We all join in for a grand jubilee!

## The Starry Gaze of Ocean's Heart

Stars above wink with glee tonight,
While dolphins play in sheer delight.
"Catch me if you can!" they yell with cheer,
As we chuckle, splashing without fear.

A fish in a tux gives quite a show,
Twirling and twirling, oh how he'd flow!
With laughter echoing deep and wide,
In the ocean's heart, we take a ride.

## A Journey Through Aquatic Veils

Bubbles rise like dreams in disguise,
With friendly squids that wear bow ties.
A jellyfish floats, looking quite grand,
While we navigate through the colorful land.

Sea turtles advise, "Just swim and glide!
Follow the current, let joy be your guide!"
And as we laugh in this shimmering sea,
Life's all about fun, just wait and see!

## Tidal Flow of Imagination

A starfish sat on the shore wide,
With thoughts of becoming a great whale glide.
"If I just had fins and a little more scale,
I'd leap through the waves and tell quite the tale!"

Beneath the blue, he chuckled with glee,
Imagining his splash would bring fish to tea.
"Oh, to swirl like a dolphin, it can't be a sin,
To wish for the magic of flippers and kin!"

But alas, he was stuck with his five squishy arms,
No fins to propel, or oceanic charms.
"Maybe I'll settle for a cool seaweed hat,
And throw fancy parties for crabs and a cat!"

So he danced with shellfish, his entourage bright,
Making waves of laughter beneath the moonlight.
In the end, it was clear as the tide ebbed low,
His dreams made him swim where reality won't go!"

## Amongst the Shadows of the Tide

In the murky depths where the sea creatures play,
A starfish declared, "I'll join the ballet!"
With a pirouette on an old piece of drift,
He twirled through the sand, oh, what a gift!

"Look at me move! I've got style, you see?
I can flipper, I can flop, I can dance with the sea!"
The fish rolled their eyes, the crabs shook their claws,
Yet the clam choir joined in with thunderous applause!

With each little flounder, he partnered with flair,
"A twirl and a splash? Just don't mess my hair!"
He chuckled and jiggled, he shimmied with pride,
"Next week I'll tackle the waves in high tide!"

They laughed till it hurt, these ocean-bound mates,
As the starfish boasted of grand future fates.
But with every new dance, he learned one strange fact:
In sea ballet, you don't want to be racked!

## Shimmering Threads of Ocean Dreams

A starfish named Larry had dreams on the sand,
To wave at the whales and be part of their band.
Yet with each little thought, he tangled his arms,
"I need glittery sequins to show off my charms!"

He strutted in circles, a glittering sight,
Telling the mollusks, "I'm ready for flight!"
With a comical flair, he donned shells for a show,
But instead of applause, the fish swam below!

"What's the secret?" he pondered with sighs,
"Maybe a top hat would open their eyes!"
With a wink and a grin, he plopped on a shell,
And danced like no creature had danced so well!

The waves roared with laughter, the crabs tapped their feet,
As Larry the starfish brought rhythm to beat.
Though not quite a whale, he sang with sheer might,
And in the ocean's dance, he found pure delight!

# The Whispering Sands of Memory

On a beach made of laughter, where dreams blend with light,
A starfish named Sam thought he'd take flight.
With the seagulls above, he plotted his quest,
"Today I'll be great, I'll outshine all the rest!"

He imagined a voyage aboard a bright shell,
Sailing the seas, oh, what stories to tell!
But he stumbled on kelp and rolled on the floor,
"Perhaps I'm more suited to beachside decor!"

So he settled with laughter, his anchor in sand,
Inviting the crabs for a ceilidh so grand.
"We'll dance and we'll giggle until break of dawn,
And I'll wear my best hat made from a prawn!"

Through sunlit adventures and shimmering tides,
Sam found joy in the fun, where silly abides.
With every lighthearted moment he'd gleamed,
He realized the best days were never just dreamed!

# Searching for Home Among the Waves

A starfish once set out to roam,
In search of a cozy ocean home.
He tried a clam, he tried a shell,
But nothing fit, oh well, oh well!

He sneezed a fish, it winked an eye,
"Ocean's big, don't be shy!"
He twirled in sand, made quite a mess,
And giggled loud in his sea dress!

He found a rock with perfect charm,
But it was cold, not warm and calm.
A crab joined in with a tiny cheer,
"Just hang with us, your friends are here!"

So starfish laughed, decided to stay,
Home's not a shell, it's friends, they say.
In tidal pools, they twirled and spun,
Best adventures, oh what fun!

## The Dreamscape of Oceanic Depths

In the depths where seaweed sways,
A starfish plotted silly ways.
He dreamed of shoes and hats so bright,
But none would fit, oh what a sight!

He tried a jellyfish for a cap,
But it just bounced, then took a nap.
A fish with fins of polka dots,
Joined in the fun, forgetting knots!

"I'll swim and dance, no time for fears,
A shoal of laughter in salty tears."
So they twirled in the ocean's light,
With starfish giggles, what a sight!

Then up a wave, they rode with glee,
Making ripples of joy, you see.
Their dreams were wild, their hearts so free,
In the ocean's arms, just let it be!

## Ripples of Imagination

One starfish woke with crafty schemes,
To ride on bubbles, chase his dreams.
He donned a mask made just of sea,
And thought, "This should be fun for me!"

With sea snails pulling at his toes,
He giggled as the current flows.
Through coral castles, under arches,
He cavorted with the playful parches!

"Oh look at me, I'm such a star!
Swimming fast, oh yes, I'll go far!"
But tripped on a crab and fell back down,
And swirled around in a comical frown!

Yet back to laughter, he did arise,
With kelp confetti, a fun surprise.
Ripples of joy in a sea of delight,
A dream that sparkles, shining bright!

## Fables of the Salted Breeze

A wise old whale told tales at noon,
Of starfish sportin' summer loons.
"Once one did wear a mermaid's crown,
And boogied till the sun went down!"

The starfish laughed, his friends all near,
"What nonsense, dear whale, but oh so clear!"
"We'll dance in the waves, with fins and flair,
And scatter laughter through the salty air!"

They leaped on bubbles, sang with glee,
Teaching fish to jig and spree.
With splashes bright, the ocean cheered,
Such fables of joy, no one feared!

"Now let's find more treasures along the way,
Dance with the tide until the end of day!"
Together they twirled, funny and spry,
Fables of breezes, where dreams fly high!

## Glimmering Wishes on the Beach

A starfish sat with quite a plan,
To swim like fish, oh yes, he can!
He wiggled his arms, gave a flick,
But ended up stuck—what a trick!

He daydreamed of being a mighty whale,
Riding the waves like a big, old gale.
But every time he tried to float,
He just sank down, what a silly goat!

With every wave, he clapped in cheer,
As crabs danced near, without any fear.
"Next time," he laughed, "I'll build a boat!"
For now, he was stuck, with dreams remote!

His friends laughed loud at his grand design,
"Floor's a sea, buddy, not a wine!"
Yet he grinned wide, glowing like a star,
Dreaming of trips to lands afar!

## The Cosmic Embrace of Shells


A conch shell said, "I'm quite the sage,
With secrets of the ocean's page.
I'll tell you tales of mermaid teas,
And how they dance with the gentle breeze!"

The starfish thought, "That sounds so neat!
I'll bring some snacks—oh what a treat!"
But when he grasped—oops! Down it fell,
The shells giggled back, could they tell?

"Your snacks are sand, oh what a blunder!
Next time just bring a jelly under!"
He pondered hard, then scratched his head,
"Perhaps I'll stick to toast instead!"

With laughter ringing among the waves,
The shell and starfish became the braves.
In cosmic dreams, they laughed all night,
Sharing whispers of sheer delight!

## Ephemeral Echoes of the Deep

Under the waves, the starfish danced,
In a world where clams had pranced.
He twirled and swirled with such delight,
But bumped a crab, oh what a sight!

"Excuse me, sir, do watch your head,
Or I might just send you off to bed!"
The crab just nodded with a grin,
"Next time, buddy, let's not spin!"

They laughed together, a crusty pair,
With bubbles drifting through the air.
The starfish joked, "You dance too slow!"
"Just take a look at my fancy show!"

Echoes carried from the bounds so deep,
Where even sea cows would giggle and leap.
In this watery land, they made a crew,
With every whirl, laughed anew!

## Reflections of a Saltwater Muse

A mirrorfish glided, sleek and sly,
"Look at me, I'm the starfish's eye!"
But the starfish rolled with quite the flair,
"Do you see that? You ain't got hair!"

With a wink, the muse gave a grin,
"I bet I can make you laugh—come in!"
They swirled and whirled, having a ball,
"Your moves are great!" the starfish called.

They bounced on waves like they were balls,
While other fish watched from their stalls.
The starfish yelled, "I'll spin so quick,
I'll be the star of this oceanic flick!"

And under the moon, they laughed and played,
In salty scenes, adventures made.
With silly tunes in bubbly streams,
Living the life of fantastic dreams!

# The Glimmering Shell's Confession

In the tide's soft embrace, I do shout,
I've seen some fish dance, without a doubt.
With bubbles of laughter, I hear their cheer,
While seagulls above jeer, so loud and clear.

Oh, the tales I could tell from the sand's warm bed,
Of crabs wearing hats, and that fish who sped.
I saw a seaweed party under the moon,
With jellyfish jiving—what a wacky tune!

But my glimmering shell, it holds secrets tight,
Like a starfish wishing, Oh what a sight!
If I had a voice, I'd sing at the shore,
Of the goofs and giggles of ocean folklore.

So when you find me, with sparkles aglow,
Remember the laughter, and let the waves flow.
For under the waves, with plenty to share,
Life's a comic strip, just come find your flair.

## When Seashells Whisper

In a conch shell's ear, a silly tale waits,
Of octopuses playing at grand dinner plates.
With jokes that they swap, oh what a delight,
While whispering secrets into the night.

Those seashells gossip, they giggle and tease,
About turtles who tumble and dance in the breeze.
A clownfish with glasses, so smart and so cool,
Tells jokes to the crabs, makes them all drool!

With each wave that crashes, a chuckle is born,
As barnacles snicker from dusk until morn.
The sea rocks, they shimmy, the driftwood does sway,
In this underwater cabaret, hip-hip hooray!

So listen close dear friend, to the ocean's deep song,
Join in the fun, you can't get it wrong.
For when seashells whisper, it's all about cheer,
A world full of laughter, so come lend an ear!

## Beneath the Glorious Horizon

Upon the bright sands, where the sand dollars play,
A crab starts a conga, hip-hip-hooray!
With sun hats and shades, they dance in a line,
Giggling and wiggling, all feeling just fine.

A dolphin does flips while the seagulls squawk loud,
Performing their acts to a shellfish crowd.
The starfish wear ribbons, all colors and flair,
As they plan a parade through the salty sea air.

From beach balls to surfboards, they join in the fun,
Building sandcastles under the sun.
But watch for the wave that comes rolling with might,
It crashes the party and sends things in flight!

Yet beneath the horizon, where laughter is grand,
The ocean keeps secrets, but we understand.
Life's a wild circus, we ride with a scream,
Join us dear friend, in this whimsical dream!

# A Voyage in Sea Glass Dreams

In a bottle afloat, there's a message so bright,
From shards of the ocean, it dances in light.
A pirate fish dangles, a spyglass in tow,
Searching for treasures where the wild currents flow.

With each tiny fragment, a story does bloom,
Of dips and of dives, like a swim in a room.
A crab with a compass, all lost in his quest,
As he took a wrong turn, still gave it his best!

The waves giggle softly, as they tease and they chant,
While clams write a melody, oh what a jaunt!
Seaglasses sparkle, like dreams on the rise,
As jellyfish tango beneath blue skies.

So come take a voyage, let your heart be your guide,
In this world of odd wonders, we splash and we glide.
For in every sea glass, a laugh does reside,
A journey of giggles that we cannot hide.

## Skimming the Surface of Tomorrow

A starfish sat upon the sand,
With hopes and dreams so grand.
He wished for feet and shoes so bright,
To dance and leap in pure delight.

A crab passed by with a wink and grin,
"What fun would that be, my finned friend?"
"Your arms are soft, your heart is light,
No need for shoes in starry night!"

He tried to skip, but just rolled back,
The waves laughed hard at his silly act.
Yet up he popped with a giggling cheer,
"Who needs to dance when you can steer?"

So with each wave, he'd twist and twirl,
Making friends in the sea, in a dizzy whirl.
Though never on two feet would he prance,
He found his joy in the ocean's dance.

## Beneath the Stars at Sea

A starfish under the moonlight beams,
Counted jellyfish, lost in dreams.
"I'd be a chef, if I had a chance,
To whip up waves in a jelly dance!"

A dolphin laughed, with bubbles around,
"A chef you are, in the deep, profound!"
"But how can one cook in the ocean's stew,
When nobody wants fish or crab fondue?"

The starfish pondered, then came to see,
"I'll just make popcorn from seaweed spree!"
With a flick and flop, he started to pop,
His friends all cheered, and they couldn't stop!

And under the stars, they snacked away,
A party erupted, without delay.
So if you look down at the waves so bright,
You might just find joy on a moonlit night!

## A Celestial Dreamscape

In a dreamscape where sea stars gleam,
A starfish fished for a sushi theme.
"With fish for rolls and seaweed wraps,
I'll host a banquet for all the chaps!"

A seahorse stared with bulging eyes,
"But you have no hands, how will you try?"
The starfish grinned, with a clever plan,
"I'll direct the waves, I'm the shellfish man!"

He twirled and spun, collecting blends,
As fish all swam, his culinary friends.
Though nothing stuck, it floated away,
They laughed and danced, a food buffet!

Then crustaceans joined with clattering claws,
A banquet formed, and loud applause.
And though the dishes went up and down,
In dream-spun madness, they wore a crown!

## With Each Wave, a New Horizon

A starfish sat with a sunburned shell,
"I wish for travel, oh wouldn't that swell?"
With each wave that splashed, he'd lurch and sway,
"The ocean's my bus, come on, let's play!"

He waved to a whale, acting quite bold,
"Take me to shores where the stories are told!"
The whale replied with a hearty laugh,
"You'd rather be here than in a draughty bath?"

"Let's surf the tides, catch that big wave,
And pretend we're pirates, bold and brave!"
But just as he plunged, he tumbled down,
Spinning and twirling, in seaweed gown!

Every splash brought a new delight,
As giggles echoed into the night.
So here he stayed, with a splash and cheer,
Loving his life, no worries near!

## The Serenity of Deep Waters

In the depths where fish do glide,
A starfish took a curvy ride.
"Why walk the sand when I can swim?
A scallop's race? Count me in!"

He twisted round a giant clam,
"Let's bake a cake, oh what a jam!"
With bubbles floating in the sea,
He laughed, "I'm more than just a key!"

A jellyfish said, "Check my moves!"
The starfish danced in flipper grooves.
"A twist! A twirl! Watch me go!"
Such joy to leap, oh what a show!

Then came a crab, with pinch and grin,
"Join my dance, let the fun begin!"
With laughter echoing throughout,
Together fun, there was no doubt.

## **Ripples of Possibility**

A starfish pondered on a wave,
"What's life like in a fishy cave?"
With thoughts of bubbles in the air,
He dreamt of jellybeans to share!

He made a friend in a bold trout,
"Let's splash around; let's swim about!"
They tried to sing a silly tune,
But fish just giggled—what a boon!

"I'll flip and twirl," he proudly said,
Then bounced right off a seaweed bed.
With every splatter and each glide,
His dreams grew big, he swam with pride!

So when the tides began to change,
He forged ahead, never felt strange.
Each ripple danced with glee anew,
For dreams were bright, and fun was true.

## Coral Gardens of the Mind

In coral gardens where thoughts bloom,
A starfish painted with a broom.
"Let's color all the sea so bright!
We'll make a splash, it's pure delight!"

A sea horse danced, all full of flair,
"Is that a rainbow I can wear?"
With every stroke, the colors spread,
Giggling fish cheered as they sped!

They mixed their blues with hints of pink,
"A masterpiece, what do you think?"
With tiny shells and bits of sand,
They filled the sea—oh, wasn't it grand!

"Let's throw a party, invite them all!"
From finned to forked, they had a ball.
The ocean floor became a spree,
In coral dreams, where fun's the key!

## Fantasia of the Oceanic Soul

In the ocean's heart, a tale unfolds,
Of starfish dreams and ocean molds.
"I'll write a story with some flair,
A fantasy of fun to share!"

With crabs as scribes and fish as muse,
They plotted tales that would amuse.
A whale with wings, what a delight,
"Oh, let's start flying, what a sight!"

A dance of bubbles, glistening bright,
In shimmering waters, pure delight.
Starfish laughed, in whirlpool spins,
Such joy found where the splash begins!

With laughter ringing through the tide,
They chased their dreams, no need to hide.
In depths of fun where fantasies roll,
An ocean of joy—the starfish's soul!

## Bioluminescent Tales of the Night

In the deep, where the jellyfish glow,
A shrimp with a flair puts on quite a show.
It dances and twirls in water so dark,
Wearing a sequined, bright neon spark.

The octopus there is a master of pranks,
Changing its colors and mimicking tanks.
It wears a tuxedo to frighten the fish,
And swims like a ghost with a mischievous swish.

Squids tell tall tales of fantastical beasts,
While clams hold their pearls, hosting underwater feasts.
A party down deep, with bubbles and cheer,
Where laughter is carried by currents so clear.

So if ever you wander through waters so blue,
Remember the antics of oceanic crew.
With giggles and bubbles, they raise quite a fuss,
In the depths of the sea, they all ride the bus.

## Whims of the Tide's Gentle Hand

The waves giggle softly as they come and retreat,
Tickling the toes of the crabs at their feet.
A seagull slides down, on the breeze it will soar,
While seaweed does ballet from the ocean floor.

With a wink and a nod, the tide plays a game,
Rolling beach balls made of sea foam, what a name!
A dolphin joins in, splashing water galore,
Causing shells to tumble and dance on the shore.

As sun shines brightly, the beach is alive,
Where sandcastles pop up, oh how they thrive!
They battle the waves in a sandy ballet,
With moats and high towers, they hope to stay.

But the tide, oh so clever, with mischief in mind,
Swoops in to reclaim what it left behind.
The shells giggle softly as they drift away,
While the sun and the stars plan their next relay.

## Constellations in a Sea of Stars

At the bottom of the sea, where the starfish reside,
They dream of the cosmos, their own cosmic guide.
With tentacles pointing, they trace out the lines,
Making constellations from seaweed and brines.

A crab named Orion wears a crown made of shells,
While the turtles tell stories where the deep magic dwells.

They navigate oceans of shimmering light,
In a whimsy-filled journey through the long, starry night.

Mermaids with flippers take flights of delight,
They giggle and swirl, under the moon's silver light.
Dancing with dolphins, through waves they do glide,
In a universe filled with joy, they abide.

So if ever you gaze at the stars from afar,
Remember the chuckles that shine like a star.
For underneath oceans, the fun never ends,
Where fish are all dreamers and laughter transcends.

# A Silhouette Against the Horizon

Along the horizon, where the sun meets the sea,
A silhouette wobbles—oh what could it be?
With a wink and a wobble, it dances in time,
Bringing laughter to waves, a whimsical rhyme.

A clam plays the drums with its shell as the beat,
While starfish in swimsuits all gather to eat.
They picnic on kelp, with sandwiches made,
For laughter erupts, in a bright ocean glade.

Their shadows grow long as the sun starts to fall,
They roll and they tumble, they giggle through it all.
With a flip and a splash, they create quite the scene,
In silhouettes dancing, just like a dream.

So next time you wander along sandy shores,
Listen closely and hear the ocean's soft roars.
For hidden in shadows, the fun will unfold,
With laughter and joy that are all tales retold.

**Wishes Cast in Coral**

A starfish sat on a rock, so grand,
With dreams of dancing in a band.
He wished for feet but had thin arms,
What charm in waves, he weaves his charms!

He tried to wiggle, he tried to sway,
But sand crabs laughed, 'that's not the way!'
With a flip and a flop, he joined the fun,
Chasing his dreams under the sun!

Fishes leaped, and they shared a laugh,
As he twirled around, a foolish path.
"Just a star," he thought, "I'll still be cool!"
Wishes are better when you're in school!

So here he prances, a curious sight,
In the coral's glow, he feels so light.
Remember, dear friends, in tides we trust,
Even starfish have wishes, it's a must!

## The Dance of Sandy Wishes

In a tidepool, a wish took flight,
A clam said, "What a silly sight!"
With a wiggle and jiggle, a sand dollar spun,
"Come join the dance, let's have some fun!"

The seaweed swayed like it had a beat,
While barnacles clapped to the rhythm so sweet.
Starfish twinkled, dreaming of fame,
Saying, "In this sea, we'll make our name!"

A jellyfish floated with a graceful cheer,
"Who needs feet when you've got sheer flair?"
With laughter and bubbles, the ocean sang,
In this sandy party, no one felt lame!

As the moon rose high and the tide played tricks,
Our wishes danced on the sea's nice licks.
So if you're ever feeling quite crummy,
Just recall the ocean, it'll make you funny!

## A Soul Adrift in the Sea


A little fish with a curious grin,
Met a starfish feeling quite thin.
"Where are you going?" the fish did prance,
"I'm off to find a seaweed dance!"

"But wait!" cried the fish, "You can't swim fast!"
"Oh pish posh," said the star, "Let's have a blast!"
So off they went, with giggles and glee,
In search of coral to climb like a tree!

They found a conch that played a tune,
As the starfish twirled under the moon.
"I'm nature's dancer!" he shouted with pride,
With ocean critters joining the ride!

But soon the tide pulled hard on their tails,
Time to go home; on this they'd set sails.
"Remember my moves!" the starfish yelled back,
"I'm sinking slowly but cut no slack!"

## Stardust on Briny Shores

On a shore with stardust beneath their fins,
A seagull cawed, "Let the laughter begin!"
A starfish giggled, "I wish for a tale,"
With seashells and sparkles upon the gale.

"Let's build a castle!" the sea turtle crooned,
As fish joined in, under sun to be swooned.
With twinkling eyes, they rolled grains of sand,
Creating a fortress, oh how grand!

A crab waved hello with a wink and a spin,
While the waves crashed in, inviting the din.
A dance-off ensued 'neath the aqua blue,
Where laughter and flippers splashed the view!

As the sun set low with its golden hue,
The starfish laughed, "Who knew I'd find crew?"
With wishes and dreams on briny shores,
Every wave whispered, "There's always more!"

## **Radiant Dreams of the Abyss**

In the deep where fish do play,
A starfish giggles all the way.
It dreams of shoes to wear so fine,
But only finds a bottle of brine.

With a wink, it wears a crown of shells,
While jellyfish dance and bubble spells.
Oh, to twirl like a mermaid queen,
But it just flips in the wave's routine.

Seaweed sways with quirk and flair,
As the starfish jokes without a care.
If only it could leap and bound,
Instead, it just sticks to the ground.

It wishes for legs instead of five,
To have a fishy high-five dive.
Yet in its heart, so bright and true,
It loves the ocean's wacky view.

## Shadows of Light in Aquatic Realms

Beneath the waves where shadows play,
A starfish dreams the night away.
It fishes for puns, oh what a catch,
In a world where sea snails hatch.

It thinks of crabs that dance in pairs,
And squeaks with laughter, without cares.
If only a squid would join the fun,
They'd prance and twirl 'til day is done.

With each wave, the laughter flows,
As seahorses whip, and seaweed grows.
In this realm of giggles and glee,
Even clams want to party, you see!

But alas, our star has but one wish,
To take a ride on a dolphin swish.
So buoyantly bright, it laughs with glee,
In this underwater jubilee!

## The Wishful Heart of the Sea

Oh, the heart of the ocean beats so bold,
Where dreams of adventures are manifold.
A starfish hopes for a hilarious fate,
To slide on a whale's back, that's first-rate!

It imagines a parade of quirky friends,
With octopus banners and jellyfish bends.
Tickling each fin with laughs so sweet,
Creating a ruckus with the flip of a feat.

In tides of joy, it snickers wide,
At sea turtles who dance, oh what a ride!
What's next on its list as it rolls with glee?
A tea party hosted by a friendly sea bee!

The starfish chuckles, takes a deep breath,
Knowing laughter's treasure outshines life's depth.
With dreams full of quirks, oh what a spree,
In salty waters, it's blissfully free.

## Murmurs of the Ocean's Quiet Dreams

Where the currents hum a silly song,
A starfish dreams, where it feels it belongs.
It wishes for wings to soar and glide,
Instead, it giggles on the ocean's tide.

With a flick of a limb, it waves to a crab,
As sea turtles tumble, oh how they blab!
"Join our conga!" they joyfully yell,
But our starfish just wishes to fit in well.

As sea anemones shake, it can barely breathe,
Each wave a chance for laughter to weave.
But who needs legs when you've got the sea?
Dance like nobody's watching, wild and free!

Beneath the shimmering, sunlit beams,
The starfish smiles while it keeps dreaming schemes.
With the ebb and flow, life's the best show,
For in giggles and play, joy will always grow.

## Journeys of the Dreaming Wave

Beneath the sea where dreams unfurl,
A wave took off—let's give it a whirl!
It met a crab, who danced with flair,
While jellyfish giggled, flipping in air.

An octopus painted a house with pride,
While clams held their shells—a cool place to hide.
The sea cucumber had a quirky hat,
And everyone laughed at the way he sat.

But a sneaky fish stole the wave's bright crest,
Said, "Don't take life too serious, just jest!"
And thus they laughed, right into the night,
For a wave without fun is a terrible sight.

So off they danced, in their watery glee,
Where dreams are the bubbles that float carefree.
With ribbits and wiggles under the tide,
The wave giggled brightly, with friends by its side.

## The Silent Call of Aquatic Spirits

In waters blue, where whispers play,
Ghostly fins would dance and sway.
A mermaid giggled, quite in a spin,
While a fish in a tux tried to do a fin.

With coral so bright, it looked like a stage,
The octopus fumbled, a little less sage.
"Watch me twist!" shouted a clam with a grin,
His pearl dropped out—oh where has it been?

A seahorse jumped, in a silly chase,
Riding the currents with grace and space.
But all of a sudden, they spied a whale's tail,
And their giggles echoed, a delightful tale.

The spirits of ocean, both silly and bright,
Play hide and seek through the gleam of the night.
With a wave and a wink, they'd assure you are free,
For who wouldn't laugh at the depths of the sea?

## Fables of the Mollusk Moonlight

At moonlight's glow, in silence they convene,
A party of mollusks, oh what a scene!
With pearls for crowns, they twirled in place,
While one little snail won the slowest race.

A clam told a joke that made everyone clap,
While an old sea turtle took a well-deserved nap.
The shrimp told secrets of tides and trends,
As laughter flowed freely, no need to pretend.

Then a starfish appeared with a twinkling grin,
Wobbly and jiggly, it spun in a spin.
The crowd erupted, it was quite a sight,
With laughter and joy, they danced through the night.

These fables of fun beneath shining stars,
Invite all the fishes from near and far.
A world full of chuckles, a splashy soirée,
In the heart of the ocean, where dreams love to play.

# Currents of Imagination Beneath the Surface

In depths of waves where giggles swirl,
A dolphin dared to challenge the whirl.
With flip and a splash, it danced with glee,
While seaweed swayed, all carefree and free.

A crab played drums on a shipwrecked box,
While the fish all danced in their matching frocks.
The bubbles rose high, like laughter in flight,
In a world full of wonders, all glittering bright.

The blowfish puffed up, quite proud of its round,
Keepsake of laughs, laughter always found.
As the clowns of the sea made the currents sway,
Inventing new games for the joyful play.

So come now, dear friends, and join in the fun,
Where imagination sparkles, second to none.
In oceans of laughter, beneath the pure light,
Let dreams take you dancing, into the night.

## The Heartbeat of the Shoreline

On the beach, a star took a nap,
With sand in its hat, did a funny little flap.
The waves whispered tales, oh so sweet,
While crabs danced around on ticklish feet.

A seagull squawked, 'What's under your shell?'
'Just dreams of fish and a cozy hotel!'
Turtles giggled, rolled over in glee,
'You've got to wake up, come join the spree!'

Laughter erupted in the sun's warm glow,
As jellyfish jived and put on a show.
"Who needs a partner? I've got this groove!"
And the starfish chuckled, finding its move.

With the tide rolling in, and beach games to play,
They splashed and they spun, oh what a day!
Under the moon, with a wink and a yawn,
A starfish's jest carried into the dawn.

## Celestial Swirls in Tidal Pools

In the pools at dusk, where the creatures reside,
A starfish wiggled with a goofy glide,
"When I grow up, I'll be a big whale!"
But then it tripped on its own floppy tail.

The sea cucumbers sighed at the sight,
"Dear star, you're fine, just stay in your light!"
Shells giggled softly, the pincher scuttled,
"Perhaps a dancer's career is befuddled?"

'Let's paint the sand with our finest hues!'
The sea urchin chimed, "I'm out of the blues!"
The star burst out laughing, "Each wave's an art,"
In tides of humor, they played their part.

With twirls and splashes, each critter took flight,
Under starlit skies, what a whimsical night!
While the world on the shore just stood still,
The cosmic delights gave the heart a thrill.

# Reflections of a Seaside Mirage

On a sunny day, tucked between the rocks,
A starfish pondered its future in flocks,
"To float or not to float, that is the plan,"
While a sea otter snacked, making a tan.

"Dear fish, have you seen my sparkling crown?"
A clam snickered loud, "You've lost your renown!"
Pufferfish puffed up, "Join our royalty!"
As the sun sparkled bright, full of loyalty.

Wave after wave, they tossed silly schemes,
"Let's start a band made of bubbles and beams!"
The starfish exclaimed, "Oh what a delight,
I'll play the sea flute, you handle the light!"

With bubbles and laughter, they filled the air,
While dolphins chortled, it was quite the affair.
As sunset painted the sky with gold,
The star took a bow, in its glory to fold.

## Beyond the Reach of the Foam

Amidst the foam, where giggles abound,
A starfish wondered, "Is this the last round?"
With seaweed in hand, it waved in delight,
While barnacles cheered, "We'll dance all night!"

On the deck of the surf, a surfer did glide,
With a splash and a laugh, like a joyful ride.
"Take that wave on, don't tumble or roll!"
The star gave a nod, "I'm in control!"

In a whirlpool of chuckles, they twirled and they spun,
As fish joined the chorus, they all were as one.
"Who needs a partner? I've got my own laugh!"
Both stars and the jelly gasped for a craft!

So with the moon glowing brightly above,
The star took a leap, full of silly love.
With each watery giggle, they soared into grace,
A merry gust flying over the place.

www.ingramcontent.com/pod-product-compliance
Lightning Source LLC
Chambersburg PA
CBHW060140230426
43661CB00003B/503